CODING UNPLUGGED

CODING WITH SCIENCE

GETTING KID-CODERS OFF THE SCREEN AND ON THEIR FEET!

BY KAITLYN SIU
ILLUSTRATED BY DAVE SMITH

We recommend adult supervision at all times while doing the activities in this book. Always be aware that craft materials may contain allergens, so check the packaging for allergens if there is a risk of an allergic reaction. Anyone with a known allergy must avoid these.

- Wear an apron and cover surfaces.
- Tie back long hair.
- Ask an adult for help with cutting.
- Check materials for allergens.

Please visit our website, www.garethstevens.com. For a free color catalog of all our high-quality books, call toll free 1-800-542-2595 or fax 1-877-542-2596.

Cataloging-in-Publication Data
Names: Siu, Kaitlyn, author. | Smith, Dave, illustrator.
Title: Coding with science / Kaitlyn Siu , illustrated by Dave Smith.
Description: Buffalo, NY : Gareth Stevens Publishing, 2026. | Series: Coding unplugged | Includes glossary and index.
Identifiers: ISBN 9781482473810 (pbk.) | ISBN 9781482473827 (library bound) | ISBN 9781482473834 (ebook)
Subjects: LCSH: Computer programming--Juvenile literature. | Coding theory--Juvenile literature. | Science--Juvenile literature.
Classification: LCC QA76.6115 S58 2026 | DDC 005.13--dc2

Published in 2026 by
Gareth Stevens Publishing
2544 Clinton St.
Buffalo, NY 14224

First published in Great Britain in 2023 by Wayland

Commissioning Editor: Grace Glendinning
Project Manager: Katie Woolley
Designer: Emma DeBanks
Illustrations: Dave Smith

Printed in the United States of America

CPSIA compliance information: Batch #CSGS26: For further information contact Gareth Stevens at 1-800-542-2595.

CONTENTS

SCREEN-FREE CODING **WITH SCIENCE**

Let's start a **CODING ADVENTURE** with **SCIENCE!** We're going to learn how to think like a computer with fun science activities you can do at home.

The activities in this book are all **UNPLUGGED**, which means you don't need a computer or a screen to learn how to code. Most of them are great to do together with friends using teamwork. Go outside if you like to get lots of fresh air!

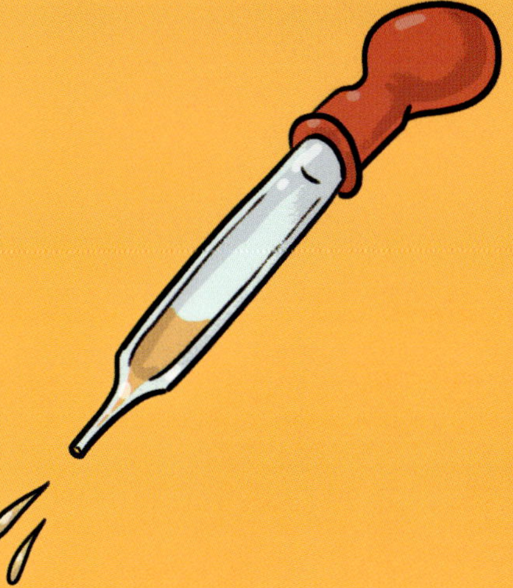

You'll be **CODING** a chain reaction, **SOLVING** a maze, and **SPOTTING** bugs in experiments (not that kind of bug!). You won't believe how much science can teach us about the key coding concepts.

GET YOUR LAB COAT ON!
THESE ACTIVITIES ARE GOING TO BRING SCIENCE AND CODING TO LIFE!

WHAT IS **CODING?**

Coding means **TALKING** to computers in their own language. Computers aren't naturally smart! A computer doesn't understand how to do *anything* unless the instructions are written in "computer code."

If a computer is asked to do a science experiment about mixing colors, it would need to be told exactly how to carry out the experiment. But first it would need to know what red and blue are! Then, we could tell it how to *create* each color and then how to mix them together.

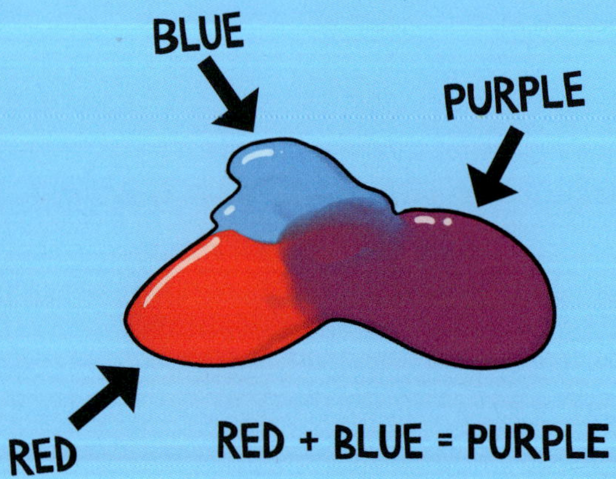

By the end of this book, you're going to be talking in **"COMPUTER SPEAK"** and will know how to give computers instructions that they will understand with some awesome science activities bringing the coding to life.

REAL-LIFE SCIENCE MADE BY CODING!

Did you know that coding is everywhere? Coding can be seen in many areas of science, such as developing vaccines, testing for diseases, and even everyday medical tests like x-rays.

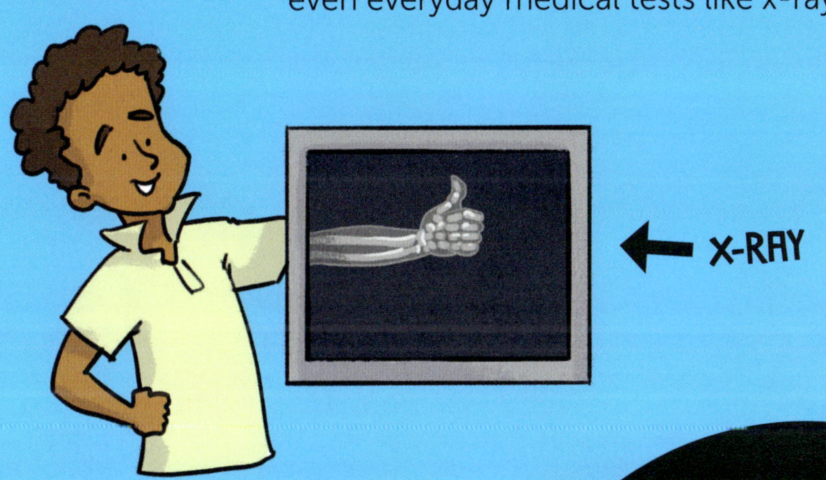

KIDS CAN CODE TOO!

You don't have to be an expert to learn to code. There are **6 SIMPLE CODING CONCEPTS** that help you to get started with coding at any age.

CODING CONCEPTS

You may know some of these already, but you can turn the page to remind yourself, or use the next few pages as quick references when you start the science **ACTIVITIES** later in the book.

KEY CODING CONCEPT #1:
THE ALGORITHM

An **ALGORITHM** is an **INSTRUCTION** given to help complete a certain task.

When performing a science experiment, an **ALGORITHM** is simply the **INSTRUCTIONS** you need to follow to complete it.

For example, when making **SLIME**, you need to follow the **ALGORITHM–OR RECIPE**–very carefully. If you measure wrong or skip a step, your slime may turn into an ooey-gooey mess!

KEY CODING CONCEPT #2:
SEQUENCE

SEQUENCE refers to the **ORDER** of steps of your algorithm.

When you give **INSTRUCTIONS**, it's important to give them in the **CORRECT ORDER**.

Sequence is very important in science experiments as well. If a scientist is working with chemical reactions, it's important they add the chemicals in the right order.

If one chemical is added out of order, it can be dangerous and could even lead to an explosion!

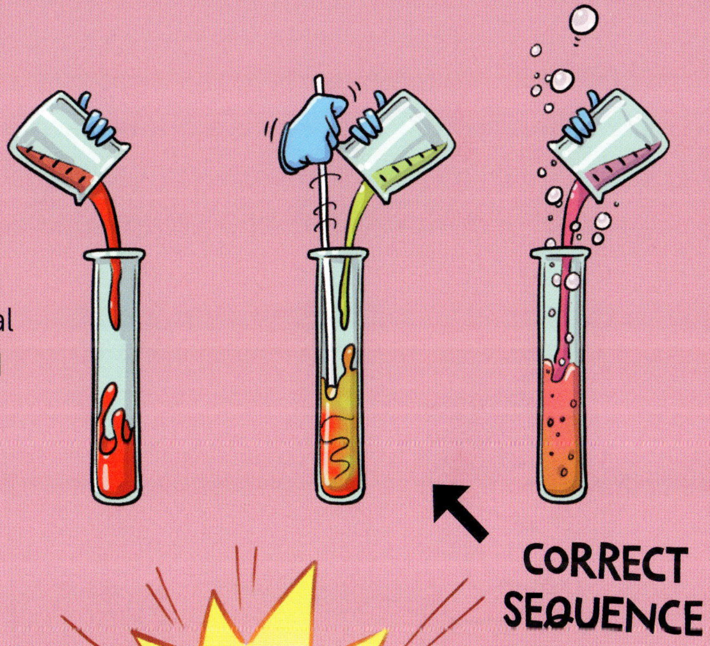

CORRECT SEQUENCE

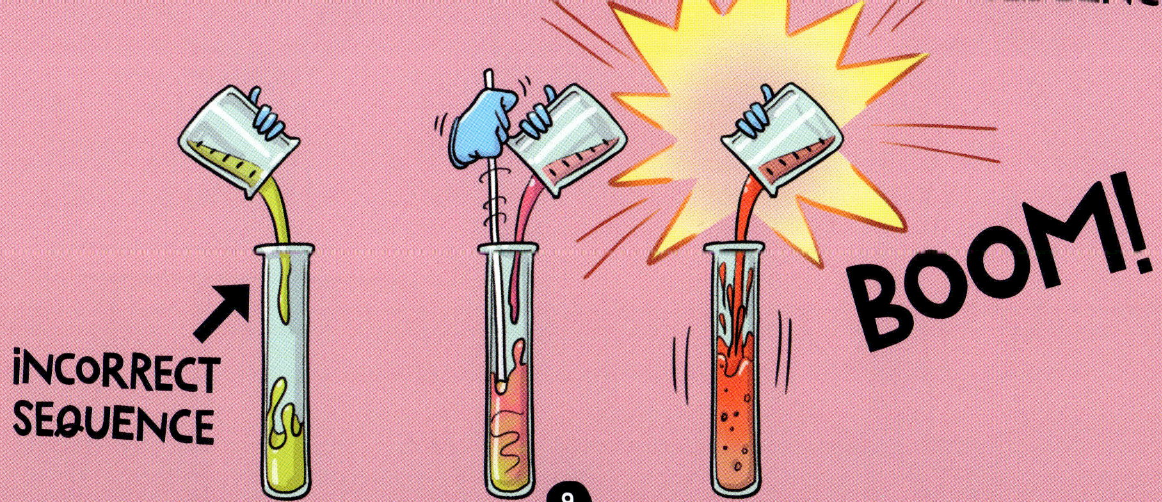

BOOM!

KEY CODING CONCEPT #3: LOOPS

A loop is a **SET** of **INSTRUCTIONS** that repeat and repeat until a specific condition is met.

The human heart is constantly **"LOOPING"** as our heart beats to keep the blood flowing to important organs in our body. In coding, we can use loops to keep the **KEY JOBS** of a computer running, just like our heart.

KEY CODING CONCEPT #4: **VARIABLES**

A variable is a way of **HOLDING INFORMATION**.
It's like a box that keeps information inside it.

Variables can be represented with **LETTERS**, **WORDS,** or **NUMBERS**.

When doing a science experiment, scientists use variables all the time to test different ideas. They may add different chemicals to their reaction to see how the results change.

KEY CODING CONCEPT #5: BRANCHING

Branching refers to making a **DECISION** based on what is **HAPPENING** or has **HAPPENED**.

In some science experiments, it's important for the temperature to be **JUST RIGHT** so that the experiment will work. So, we make decisions depending on the temperature of the liquid we're working with. For example, if it's getting **TOO HOT**, then we might turn **DOWN** the flame. If the temperature is **TOO COLD**, then we might turn it **UP**. This choice is called a **BRANCH**.

KEY CODING CONCEPT #6: **DECOMPOSITION**

Decomposition refers to breaking something up into **SMALLER PARTS**.

It's helpful to decompose a big coding (or science!) problem by **UNDERSTANDING** all the **SMALLER BITS** that make it up.

LIGHT

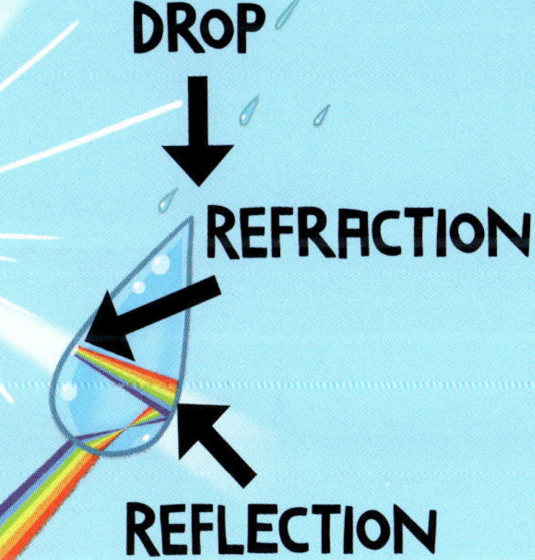

It's a bit like a raindrop **BREAKING UP** white light to show all its many parts, as a rainbow!

OBSERVER

Do you know all the **COLORS** that are mixed together to make **WHITE LIGHT**?

SEQUENCING UNPLUGGED: CODE A RUBE GOLDBERG MACHINE

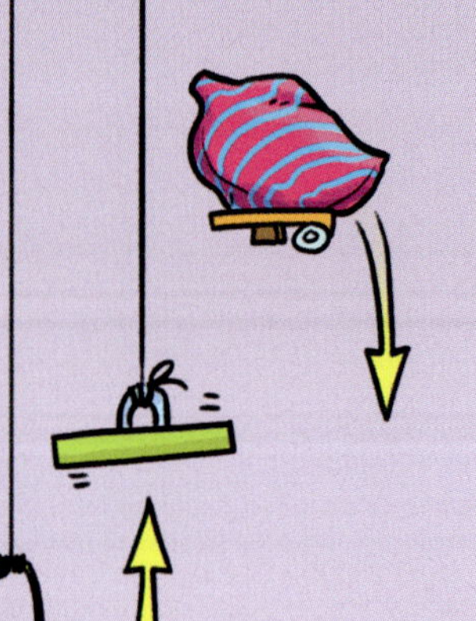

A Rube Goldberg is a **MANY-STEP MACHINE**, or a **CHAIN REACTION**. It is used to help complete a simple task, such as pouring a glass of water or turning off a light.

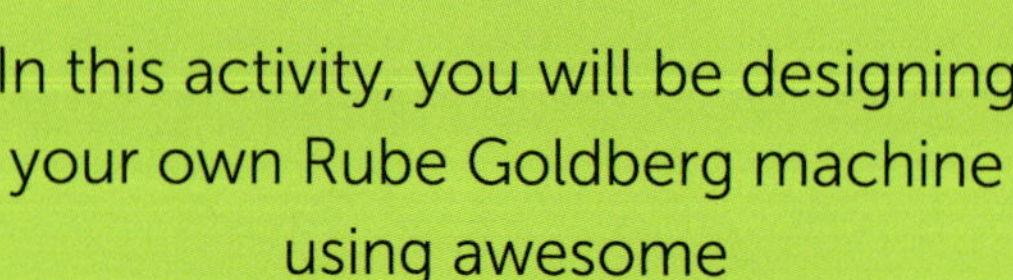

In this activity, you will be designing your own Rube Goldberg machine using awesome **CODING KNOWLEDGE**. We'll practice careful **SEQUENCING**, and even have a chance to **DEBUG** at the end.

WARNING

WARNING: Scientists and coders alike must be very careful and should have the help of an adult when putting together and performing an experiment with moving parts or reactions.

MATERIALS YOU WILL NEED:

- Kitchen roll or toilet roll tubes
- Books or cardboard
- Water bottles
- Dominoes
- Toy cars
- Tins or containers that can roll
- String
- Marbles
- Toothpicks and balloons (if balloon-popping is a goal)
- Any other interesting materials you might find to build a machine (with permission)!

WHAT WILL YOUR MACHINE DO?

First, choose a **GOAL** for your Rube Goldberg machine.

Examples of goals could be:

Turning a switch
ON or **OFF**

CLOSING
a door

POURING WATER
onto a plant

POPPING
a balloon

SEQUENCE YOUR CHAIN REACTION **ALGORITHM**

Now it's time to design your chain reaction algorithm, using a careful sequence!

In Rube Goldberg machines, the **SEQUENCE** of the instructions is very important. As these machines use chain reactions, the steps **MUST** happen in order for your machine to work.

Write out **EACH STEP** in the **CHAIN REACTION** on a piece of paper, in order, to **COMPLETE** your algorithm design.

Here are some ideas of **CHAIN REACTION STEPS** you could include in your project.

You can start with **THREE SIMPLE STEPS** in your chain reaction for this project.

IDEA 1

A marble dropping down a paper towel tube as a chute.

IDEA 2

Dominoes falling in sequence.

IDEA 3

A car rolling down a ramp.

IDEA 4

Two cups connected by a pulley. When a marble drops into the cup the pulley is activated.

IDEA 5

Car with a toothpick taped onto the roof, popping a balloon.

GAME PLAY: TEST YOUR MACHINE

Now that you have your Rube Goldberg algorithm written, it's time to **TEST** your machine. **BUILD** your sequence and **TRY** your chain reaction.

WARNING

WARNING AGAIN! Any liquids, heavy, or sharp objects should only be handled with guidance from an adult.

GAME PLAY: DEBUGGING!

Did your machine work? It's **NORMAL** to not get it perfect the first time. The same is true for coders. When coders make **MISTAKES**, they need to **DEBUG** their program.

Look at your machine design and make some **ADJUSTMENTS** so that the chain reaction will work. Or do you need to **REPLACE** or **REMOVE** one of the steps entirely? Think like a scientist and run lots of tests to get the bugs out!

SPOT THE CODE!

Spot the code! A scientist in the lab is planning an experiment measuring the temperature of chemical reactions. Here is her "recipe" card for this experiment. Let's spot the coding concepts she's using.

SPOT THE LOOPS!

This experiment requires two loops. Which steps show them?

1. Add 1 tsp from the red test tube to the beaker.
2. Add 2 tsp from the green test tube to the beaker.
3. Add ½ tsp from the orange test tube to the beaker.
4. Repeat steps 1–3, then move on to Step 5.
5. Measure the temperature.
6. If it's below 60°F (15°C), then turn on the flame.
   If it's above 60°F (15°C), then add a small ice cube.
7. Add 1 tsp from the yellow test tube to the beaker.
8. After five minutes, measure the temperature again and record it in a chart.
9. Repeat step 8 five more times.
10. Turn off the flame when finished.

SPOT THE BRANCH!

This experiment has a branch in its recipe. Can you spot it?

SPOT THE BUG!

The scientist made a mistake in her algorithm. Can you spot it?

(ANSWERS ON PAGE 48)

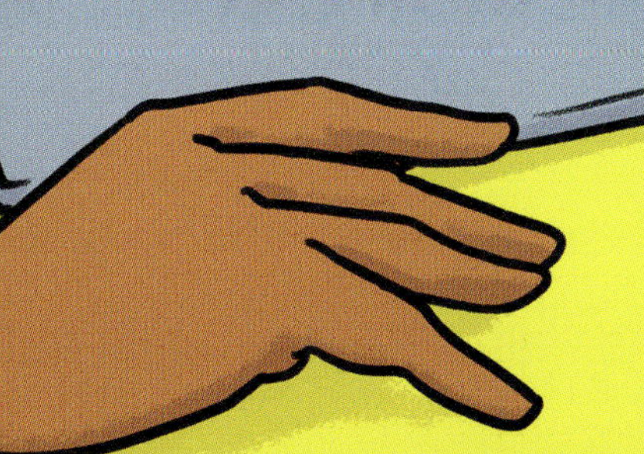

VARIABLES AND LOOPS UNPLUGGED: CODE YOUR OWN SCIENCE EXPERIMENT

Let's have fun with a classic and fun science experiment. In this activity, we are going to create our own volcano and use our coding concepts at the same time!

This unplugged coding activity will teach us how **VARIABLES** and **LOOPS** can program different outcomes for each experiment.

WARNING

WARNING: Careful science alert! You should have the help of an adult when putting together and performing an experiment with reactions and possible allergens. If you are allergic to any of the ingredients, you should not use it.

MATERIALS YOU WILL NEED:

- Large empty plastic bottle
- Warm water
- Dish soap
- White vinegar
- Baking soda
- Red food coloring
- An adult to help you!
- Some optional modeling clay or card to build up the shape of a volcano around your bottle.

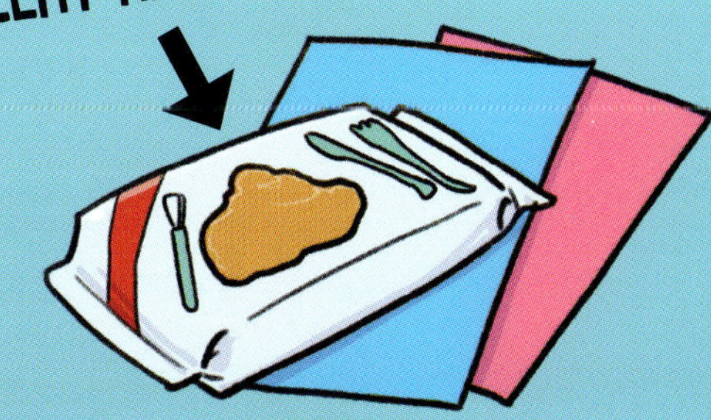

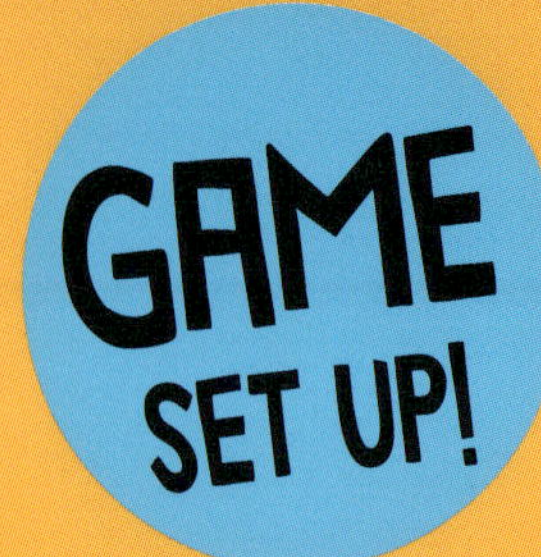

In this activity, you will be following a **VOLCANO ALGORITHM**. We are going to use the concept of variables and loops to **MAKE CHANGES** to our algorithm and **TRACK** the results.

In this science experiment, we can change the amount of baking soda **(THE VARIABLE)** to change the results of the eruption.

Also, when we add drops of food coloring, we are actually performing a loop:

What do you think will happen if you put in only one drop of food coloring, compared to **FIVE** drops?

You can code your own set of two volcanos, or run this experiment alongside a **FRIEND**, who uses a different volcano code!

VOLCANO **ALGORITHM**

1. Mix 2 tsp (10 ml) of dish soap, 1 1/4 cups (300 ml) of vinegar and 3/4 cup (200 ml) of water in your bottle.

2. Now it's time to use our coding skills to program different variables and loops in the algorithm. Code your own **"ERUPTION"** liquid:

Mix ½ cup of water with the following choices:

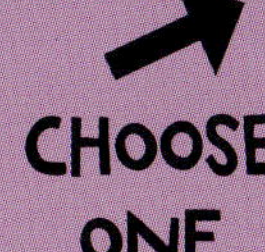

BAKING SODA VARIABLE

1/4 cup baking soda
1/3 cup baking soda
1/2 cup baking soda

LOOP VARIABLE

1 drop red food coloring
3 drops red food coloring
5 drops red food coloring

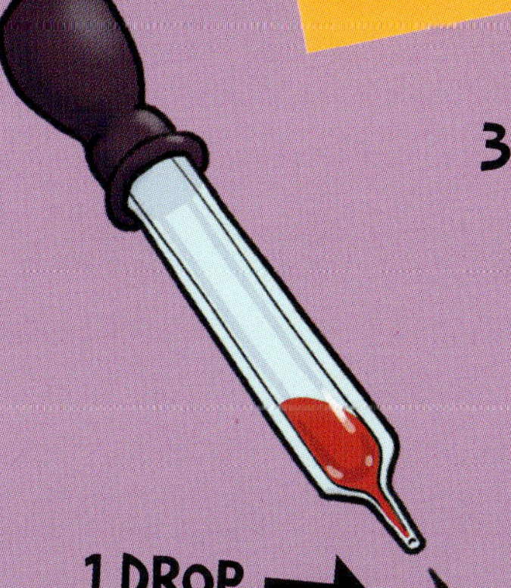

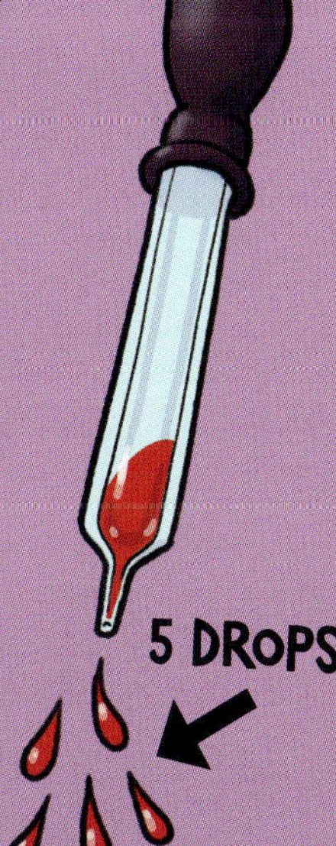

Now it's time to **RUN** your experiment. Create your **FIRST VOLCANO** with your chosen baking soda variable and food coloring loop.

1. Add your eruption liquid **QUICKLY** to the bottle.

2. Enjoy the results!

WHOOSH!

Once this is complete, wash out your bottle and do the experiment **AGAIN** with a new set of **VARIABLES** and **LOOPS**. Or, if you did this with a friend, start **COMPARING RESULTS** now.

What were the **DIFFERENCES** you noted? Were there more bubbles with **MORE** or **LESS** baking soda?

What was the effect of adding **MORE** or **LESS** food coloring?

Make notes of how changing your **CODE** affected the eruption.

DECOMPOSE THIS!

Take a look at this amazing water sample, as it appears under a microscope! So many interesting **CREATURES** to look at. But how many of each are in this sample? Be a scientist and decompose this complicated picture.

(ANSWERS ON PAGE 48)

HOW MANY
CAN YOU SPOT?

ALGORITHMS UNPLUGGED: CODE YOUR OWN MAZE

In this activity, you will create a maze of underground "burrows" and code a selection of stuffed animals through it. You'll need to practice your algorithm design skills to complete the activity.

In this activity, the **"PROGRAMMER"** will need to give the animals a set of instructions to guide them through the maze.

LET'S GET BUILDING!

MATERIALS YOU WILL NEED:

- Large piece of cardboard (as big as you can find! The larger the cardboard, the more complicated and difficult your maze burrows can be!)
- Marker
- Pencil
- Ruler
- 2 to 3 small stuffed animals

To set up the game you will need to design a maze on your board.

* **DIVIDE** your cardboard into a grid with **SQUARES** that are about the same size as the biggest stuffed animal you'll be using.

* Draw a maze with marker on your cardboard. Use the grid lines to act as guides for the maze. Don't forget to make lots of **DEAD ENDS**!

Mark one corner as the **START**, where all the animals will enter "the burrow."

* Mark a **HOME** for each animal on the grid.

* Place your first animal in the **START** position.

* Get a blank piece of paper to write out your **ANIMAL ALGORITHMS**.

* Write directions for each animal to get from **START** to **HOME**.

AN EXAMPLE MIGHT BE:

CRAWL **TWO** SPACES **RIGHT**
THEN CRAWL **TWO** SPACES **UP**
THEN CRAWL **THREE** SPACES **RIGHT**

* When you think you've planned the **SEQUENCE** properly, it's time to **CALL OUT** your algorithms!

* Have a partner act as your **ASSISTANT** and move each animal along the maze to their home!

Did your animals get to their homes on the first try? If you made a mistake, don't worry! **MISTAKES** are an **IMPORTANT PART** of **CODING**. You'll just need to **DEBUG** your algorithms and **TRY AGAIN**!

TRY
AGAIN!
HMMMMM!

SPOT THE BUG!

DNA in our bodies makes us who we are by following a code—a very careful algorithm. Find the error in the DNA code that could cause a big mix-up!

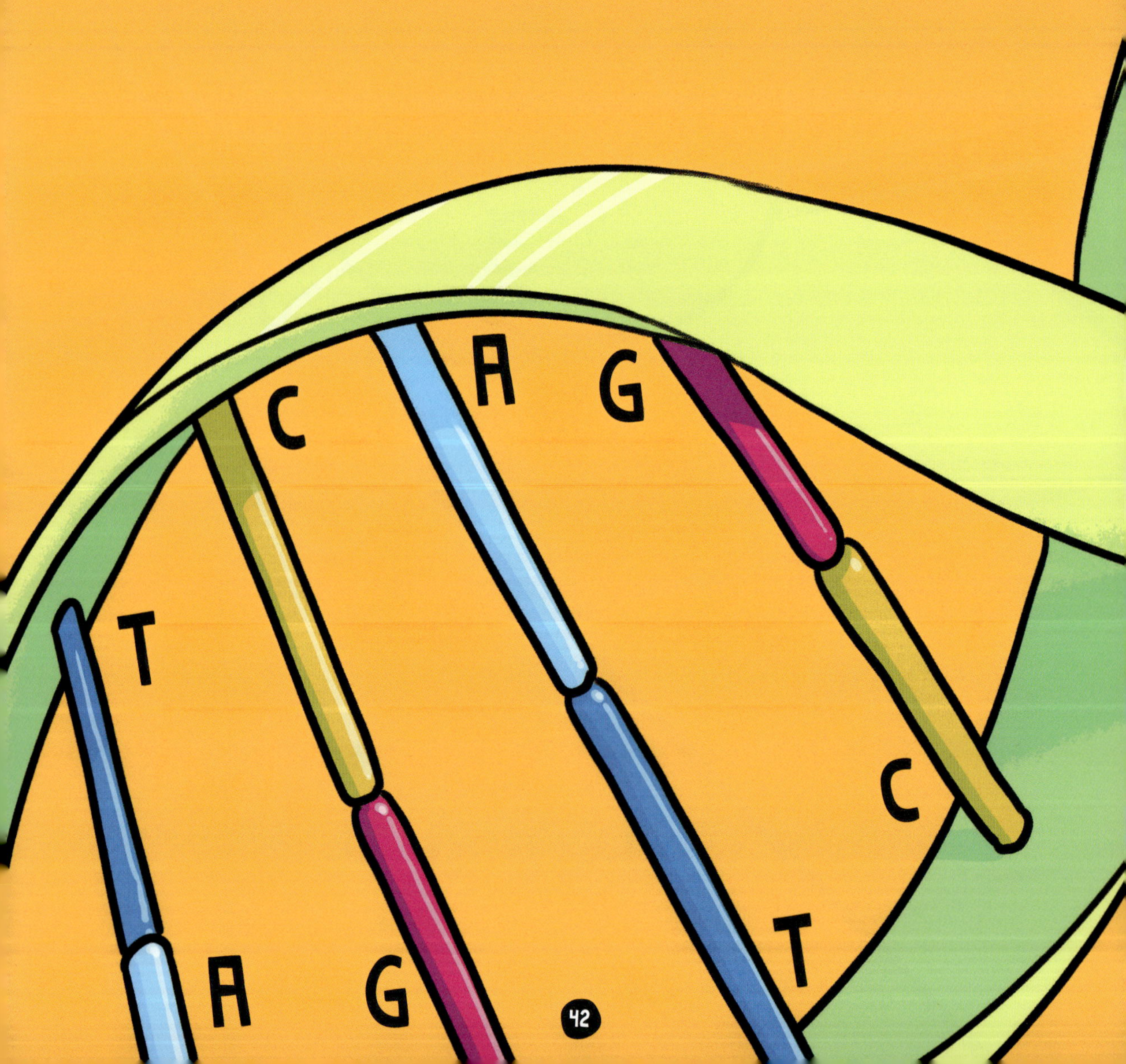

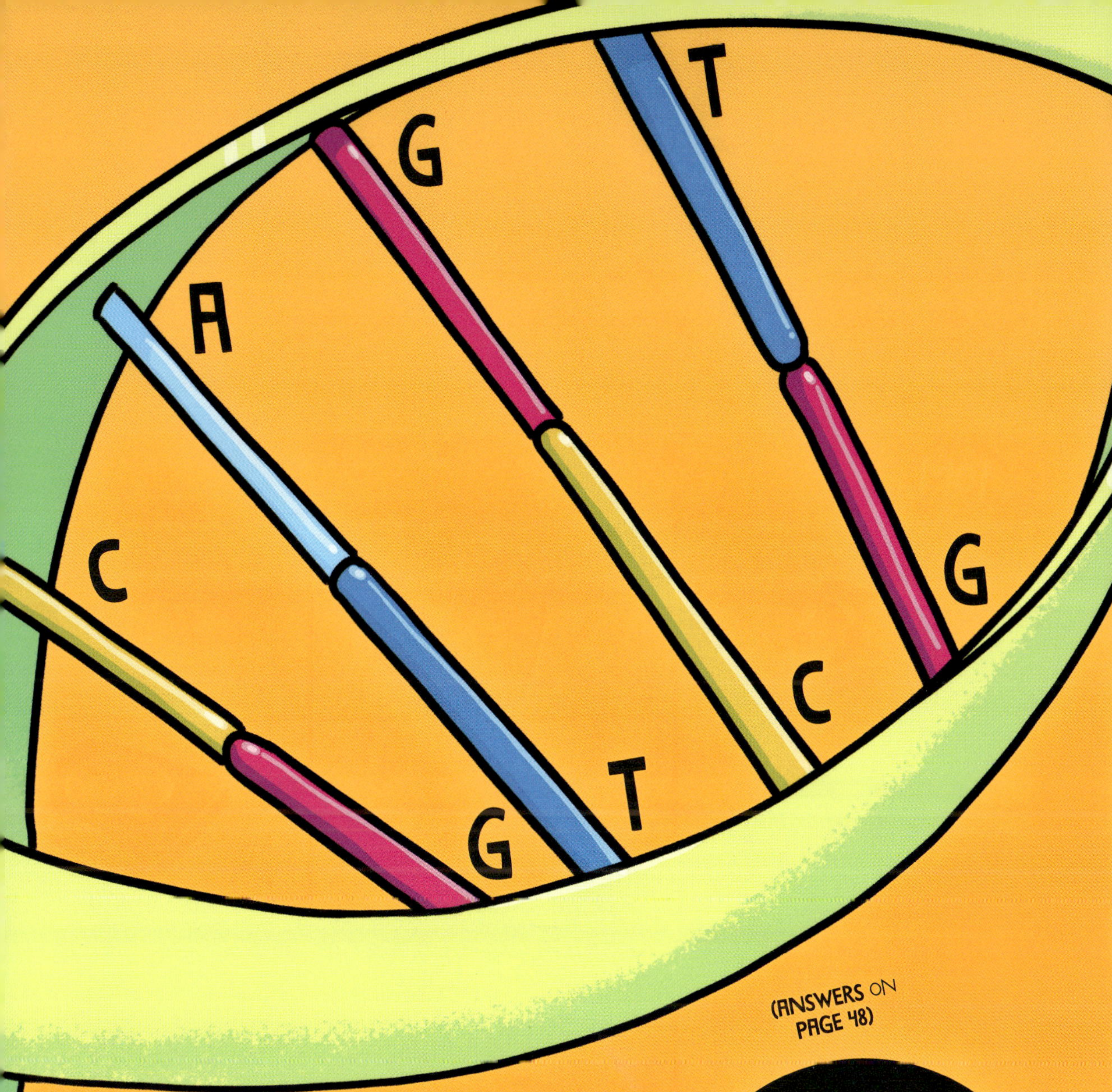

(ANSWERS ON PAGE 48)

BASE PAIRS

A = PALE BLUE T = BLUE
C = YELLOW G = PINK

C ALWAYS PAIRS WITH G
A ALWAYS PAIRS WITH T

LET'S **SOLVE A CODING PUZZLE!**

We've now learned the basic concepts of coding and we are ready to think just like a computer.

TOM

 (Tom)		Oxygen **O**
Hydrogen **H**		
Gold **Au**	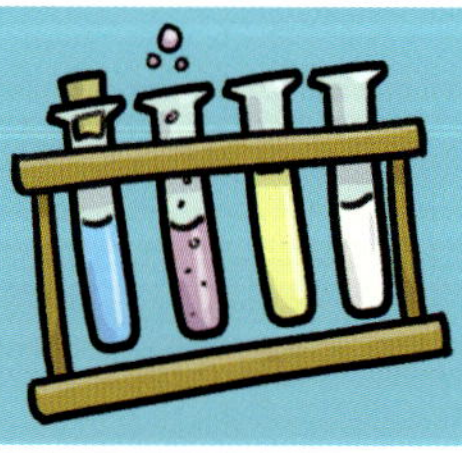	Sodium **Na**
	Oxygen **O**	Neon **Ne**

Write an algorithm to collect atoms to make:

1. A water molecule: 2 hydrogen atoms and 1 oxygen atom
2. Salt: 1 sodium atom and 1 chlorine atom

In this puzzle, we'll need to use our coding skills to solve a periodic table maze.

Help Tom gather the elements he needs to make molecules without running into any obstacles.

Write out the algorithm on a separate piece of paper.

	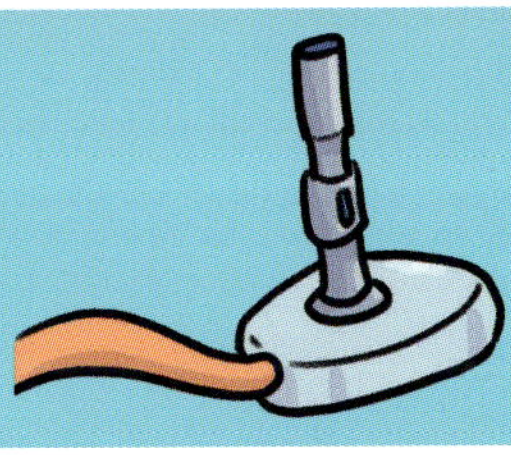	Carbon C
Potassium K	Hydrogen H	Calcium Ca

	Chlorine Cl	

THINK LIKE A COMPUTER!

GLOSSARY

ALGORITHM: An algorithm is an instruction given to help complete a certain task.

BRANCH: Branching refers to making a decision based on what is happening or has happened.

CHAIN REACTION: A set of events where the outcome of each event causes the next one.

DEBUG: Find and solve a problem in coding instructions.

DECOMPOSITION: Breaking down problems into smaller steps.

EXPERIMENT: A test done to learn something or confirm a hypothesis.

LOOP: A set of instructions that repeat until a specific condition is met.

REFLECTION: Heat, light, or an image that bounces off an object or surface.

REFRACTION: When light changes direction, or bends, and it moves from one material to another.

SEQUENCE: The order of steps.

VACCINE: An injection given to activate the immune system and protect against specific diseases.

VARIABLE: A way of holding information. It's like a box that keeps information inside of it.

NOTES FOR ADULTS

WHY CODING UNPLUGGED?

Teaching kids to code is a great way to introduce them to the basics of programming and have them learn problem-solving, logic, and critical thinking skills. These skills are applicable in real life, in school, at work, or even while they're playing video games!

One of the best ways to begin coding is to learn to code **UNPLUGGED**, so no computer or other hardware is required! By taking coding offline, it's easy to focus on the basic concepts, which are fundamental to learning to code. Combining coding learning with creative or physical activities is a great way to embed the information and keep children active.

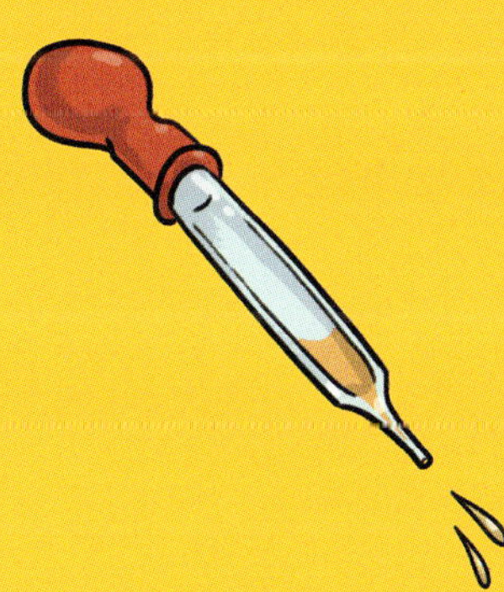

FURTHER INFO

FOR MORE FUN CODING BOOKS, WHY NOT TRY ...

Bell, Samantha. *Coding Algorithms.* Minneapolis, MN: Kids Core, an imprint of Abdo Publishing, 2024.

Kulz, George. *Coding Variables.* Minneapolis, MN: Kids Core, an imprint of Abdo Publishing, 2024.

ANSWERS

PAGE 23:

Step 4 and 9 represent a loop, which is a step that repeats until a certain condition is met.

Step 6 represents a branch. The next step in the experiment depends on the temperature.

Step 7 is the bug as there is no test tube with yellow liquid.

PAGE 33:

5 stars
8 circles
5 triangles
5 long ovals
7 short ovals

PAGE 43:

The farthest base pair to the right represents an error in the DNA code with T incorrectly pairing with G.

PAGE 45:

Option for Algorithm 1:
Down 1, collect hydrogen
Down 2
Right 1, collect oxygen
Right 1,
Up 1
Right 1
Up 1
Right 1, collect hydrogen

Option for Algorithm 2:
Down 3
Right 2
Up 1, collect sodium
Down 1
Right 2, collect chlorine